LUXURY HOMES AND LIFESTYLES

Elements for the New Millennium

LUXURY HOMES AND LIFESTYLES

Elements for the New Millennium

IDEAS, CONCEPTS and STRUCTURES

by

Orren Pickell

Principal Photography by Linda Oyama Bryan

Published by
The
Ashley
Group

Published by The Ashley Group
A Cahners® Business Information Company
42 Sherwood Terrace, Suite 1
Lake Bluff Illinois 60044

Printed in Hong Kong

Concept and Design by Paul A. Casper

ISBN 0-9642057-4-2

First Edition

Acknowledgments

My thanks to the homeowners who graciously allowed us
to photograph their homes for use in this book. Special thanks to the talented
craftsmen whose work appears in the photos:

Martin Associates Landscaping

Paul Heath Audio & Video

Richard Menna Interior Design Ltd.

and

Wood-Mode Fine Custom Cabinetry

Contents

Introduction

The excitement of the 21st century is upon us. The music, art, fashion, and home design of the late 1990's and early 2000's will soon appear in retrospectives under the heading "Turn of the Century Style." The homes we're designing this afternoon will be examples of early 21st century architecture and design. The future is already here. The seeds of the future are already planted. It's a unique time to be building or designing a home. This book represents our company's vision of what building and designing a home in the 21st century will be like. I have been in the home-building profession for over 30 years. I've seen major changes in the way people use their kitchens, the emergence of the Great Room and the first-floor master suite. I've seen preferences for room sizes expand and contract, the trends toward open space and small, intimate space. But the one trend that I believe will be truly lasting and revolutionary is the design/build approach to the processes of building and remodeling. The idea of bringing together the talents of the architect, builder, and entire team under one business roof is so logical, simple, and economical that it will be the accepted model for many years to come. We've identified nine main elements that form the design/build process. They are each individually important, but together, represent an approach that serves clients better than anything that has preceded it. The superior results of the process are evident in the photographs and illustrations that are included in these pages. Design/build produces quality, luxury, beauty, and the creative experience of a lifetime. Now and well into the future.

—Orren Pickell

Time is of the Essence
The Design/Build Approach

The most valuable commodity at the end of the 1900s is time. Many of the families

we meet in our business tell us so. There's not enough time to get all of their

work done at the office. Not enough time to pick up the dry-cleaning and make it to

their tennis match or the kids' athletic events between 3 and 5 o'clock. And

certainly not enough time to coordinate the efforts of six or seven professionals who are

working on their new home or kitchen remodeling project. That's why the idea

of design/build, a streamlined approach to getting a home built, is the defining trend we

see for the new millennium.

I've watched the idea of design/build evolve over the years that I've been in the

home-building business, from a time when an architect and builder were

usually hired separately on a project and only occasionally worked harmoniously

for the good of the client. Today, more and more firms have recognized

the value of bringing the architect and builder together from the very beginning.

Its appeal lies in its simplicity: One source for their project. One team

that has proven success working together. One pay structure to understand and

control. It's simply the easiest way to get a custom home built.

We've learned from our clients that building a beautiful new home is

one of life's great milestone events. In their minds, it's not a process to

be managed, but an experience to be relished. When people look at blueprints,

they see their hopes for the future and their plans for their families, not

a set of technical working documents. They are excited and happy, as well they

should be. When they go to sleep at night, they want to be dreaming

about move-in day, not tossing and turning over a spat between the interior

designer and the builder, or how high costs are getting on all the

different budgets involved in the project. So they like design/build for its ability

to take the frustration and stress out of the experience.

"Not only does this Prairie-style dining room double as a formal or informal eating area, but it is surrounded by cabinets. Cabinetry is one of the prime contributors to the beauty *and* functionality *of a home."*

Dave Heigl, Partner, CabinetWerks

"It's a privilege *to work closely with the client as a team and* create *the atmosphere that suits their lifestyle."*

Orren Pickell

" *One of the most gratifying comments we hear from clients is that they found the home-building process very 'manageable.' That's the main* benefit *of design/build. It's a process that's efficient and effective. And it doesn't sacrifice quality.*"

Tony Perry, *Vice President, Design Group*

"Clients who are new to the design/build philosophy are surprised *and delighted to find all of the professionals talking to each other and being orchestrated in one place. And they appreciate their status as a critical contributor to the evolving design of their home."*

Wendy Cohen, *Vice President of Sales and Marketing*

"This kitchen incorporates so many aspects of the design/build process: stunning design, quality materials, exquisite *craftsmanship...all come together to meet the specific needs of the client."*

Dave Heigl

"There are so many decisions to be made when building a home — to a client it can seem overwhelming. Design/build takes the pressure off the homeowner by making the decisions manageable, while at the same time ensuring that no detail has been overlooked. For the client, choosing details like the wrought iron railing and limestone floor becomes a source of excitement *rather than a source of anxiety.".*

Orren Pickell

More and more, people want to have a great creative experience building

their house! Despite horror stories that float around dinner parties

and soccer fields, people optimistically believe that the experience

can and should be fun. They're right.

People have problems when the right teams aren't working on the project. By

this I mean the teams don't communicate well with their client, or with

one another. This is where

design/build really shines.

By placing the architect and

builder on the team from

the beginning of the project,

working in the same office,

homeowners are relieved of the

difficult and sometimes

frustrating task of finding a builder

and an architect on their

own. The design/build firm brings in other professionals appropriate to the

project, like an interior designer, landscape architect, and kitchen

designer, if they're not on staff already. In other words, a lot of the tough, time

consuming, and oftentimes fruitless footwork is taken out of the

experience, leaving the clients free to immerse themselves in the creative

pleasures of designing a home.

Today and tomorrow, I believe people will continue to prefer the design/build

approach because it's the easiest, most logical way to custom-build a

home. And it's sure to save them their most precious commodity — time.

One of Life's Greatest Delights

The Entertainment Element

Today's luxury home customers are changing the rules of the game.
They expect the process of designing and building their dream home
to be fun. And they're right. When people are investing the time
and resources required to build at the custom level, they're
entitled to an entertaining, educational, and
enriching experience.

When the architect, builder, landscape architect, and interior designer all

join the team early on, the client has the chance to develop

relationships with the team members that can last a lifetime. They need to know

and like each other. The resulting cross-pollination of ideas leads to

truly original, imaginative thinking. The clients gain access to a larger variety of

concepts and have more time to review them. Good design/build teams

know how to keep the process moving forward in a positive, enjoyable way. The

collaborative focus allows them to develop an intimate concentration of

purpose and give the client a high degree of personal attention.

Designing and building firms keep customers emotionally involved by

making the whole process entertaining. Why shouldn't it be? It's

exciting, totally absorbing, and adventurous. If someone is investing the time

and resources to make their vision of a dream home come alive, they

deserve — and expect — to have a wonderful time doing it.

"Designing dining areas is one of the most enjoyable steps in the process for homeowners. We encourage them to think of

ways to make efficient use of the space. A dining room is like a jewel *or a piece of art. It should be admired and*

enjoyed every day. This dining area, for instance, can be used daily, because it is either casual or elegant, depending upon

the occasion and the whim of the homeowners. Because it is flexible, it is used regularly, so it demands a stunning view."

Orren Pickell

"People love the experience of using the computer to 'see' the possibilities we can integrate into their new home. The architectural elements in this home were really fun *to design—not only for the clients, but for me and the design staff as well."*

Tony Perry, *Vice President, Design Group*

"A sophisticated client, and the children, have been to plays, movies, concerts, and sporting events in some of the finest facilities in the world. They demand high-quality distributed audio and video throughout the home that duplicates the experience they've grown used to. They also want the flexibility to remotely control these entertainment *systems from anywhere in the house."*

Dave Kapor, *Paul Heath Audio & Video*

"My philosophy as an interior designer is, 'Give the client what they want.' I designed the room using an antique armoire that the client already owned as a starting point. The client couldn't wait to see the result! It was such an enjoyable *event for both of us."*

Richard Menna, *Richard Menna Interior Design*

The authentic French poster dominates the room and is really an expression *of the client's tastes. The homeowner searched out and bought this poster, and I found the framer. The level of involvement that the design/build approach offers the client always leads to wonderful things."*

Richard Menna

"Our design team redefined *the use of space in this room. By centralizing it in the home, we transformed*

it into a less formal area that can be used daily. Formal or informal, it looks contemporary and sleek."

Tony Perry

"As in architecture, unique details that are integrated into a landscape design contribute to its overall success and character.

Water is a key element that can be an endless source of pleasure as it animates and brings a garden to life."

James P. Martin, Landscape Architect, Martin Associates Landscaping

One way to make the process entertaining is to leverage the power of technology. For example, early in the design process, the design/build firm might surprise its clients with an animated, virtual reality video presentation of their developing project. It's a fun way to better visualize the interiors and make changes and adjustments before construction begins.

Once all decisions are finalized, the clients receive a final automation video that they can enjoy showing to their friends and family. Clients are also invited to the firm's offices for computerized virtual "fly-bys" of their home. The technology allows for an element of play and wonder that enhances the home-building experience for everyone involved. From personal experience, I know that it's great to hear the people on the design staff laughing with clients while they "fly" through the living room and down the hall to the bedroom. The joy is contagious!

Design/build firms keep the process lively by being organized, efficient, and sensitive to the needs of the client. This even includes the bidding period, a normally quiet time when clients warily await the final costs of the materials and finishes they have chosen. Someone from the team stays in touch to keep them calm, interested, and continually attuned to what's being done on their behalf.

"The kitchen is once again the family gathering place. By taking this into consideration using the design/build approach, the family's needs can be incorporated to create a practical and beautiful layout. As a result, it will be a comfortable space that all the family members will enjoy."

Baroque Fineberg, *Wood-Mode Fine Custom Cabinetry*

Enriching the Mind
and Spirit
with Knowledge
The Learning Element

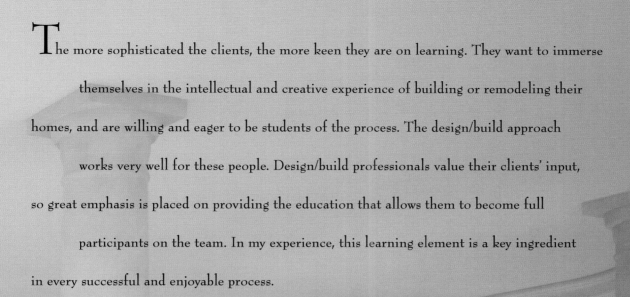

The more sophisticated the clients, the more keen they are on learning. They want to immerse themselves in the intellectual and creative experience of building or remodeling their homes, and are willing and eager to be students of the process. The design/build approach works very well for these people. Design/build professionals value their clients' input, so great emphasis is placed on providing the education that allows them to become full participants on the team. In my experience, this learning element is a key ingredient in every successful and enjoyable process.

Building a home, adding a first floor master bedroom, or renovating a

kitchen are common projects for designers and builders. Clients almost

always come to the project with a mixture of joy and apprehension. There are

many decisions to be made and dollars to be spent. The final result is

long term, if not permanent. Unless the clients have built other homes in the

past, or are in the building profession themselves, their apprehension is

fueled by the fact that they lack the knowledge to make these decisions. This

lack of knowledge is what you'll find at the root of the home building

horror stories often heard on golf courses and in supermarkets. Smart,

sophisticated, successful people who are well educated in their own

fields run into all manner of crises in the custom home building process. They

choose an exquisite flooring material, but will it perform well under the

daily onslaught of young children and two or three dogs? They opt to build a

fourth bedroom to use as an office space, but fail to realize that signifi-

cant wiring for phone and electrical lines, as well as TV and modem

cables, must be installed in a modern office. They decide to wait on

designing a landscape without realizing how disappointed they'll feel when the

exterior doesn't enhance their beautiful new home or addition. These

kinds of problems are altogether avoidable when the client is educated and

guided by a professional team.

"Design/build creates as much satisfaction for us as it does for the client. Designing this foyer

and seeing the project all the way through to completion, knowing that it's exactly what the client

wanted...it's a source of enormous satisfaction for us."

Tony Perry

"We had such fun *educating the client in designing this home office. By the time we made the final materials selections, they were so excited about their choices and combinations of wood, stone, carpet and space planning, I knew they'd be delighted with the end results."*

Dave Heigl

"I love this view. It's so **elegant** and timeless. There were a lot of people involved in

the process of designing and building this setting. They're all extremely proud of it."

Orren Pickell

Design/build offers an opportunity for a learning element that is simply

unavailable to clients who hire a separate architect, contractor, designer,

and landscape architect to work on their home. First, there is simply more time

for client education, since less time is required in assembling the team.

One firm might have financial and legal experts to handle the paperwork,

interior designers, experienced building and construction crews, award-

winning architects, master craftsmen in cabinetry, carpentry, and detailed

woodworking, and superintendents to oversee their work.

Second, the client is a member of the design/build team,

not a team coordinator. When the professionals are one

working unit, the need for clients to take on team

management disappears. The considerable time and

energy that might have been put toward juggling timelines,

deadlines, change orders, and managing personality

clashes can now be put toward learning about architectural

details or room layouts or the pros and cons of granite

countertops.

Finally, the design/build process encourages homeowners

to become passionate about their homes. As full mem-

bers of a team that has designed and built each special detail together...as

educated homeowners who understand why materials and architectural

and landscaping elements were chosen... clients are enriched with first-hand

knowledge. They become co-authors of an enduring art form.

The education process starts early, when the client is first deciding whether or not to custom-build. At the time of the client's first meeting, company representatives have already visited the proposed home site. From their measurements and observations of the property, these professionals begin to educate clients on its possibilities. It may turn out that the initial visit sparks new, better ideas.

As the project begins, design/build professionals interview clients extensively to learn their personal preferences. They are quizzed in ways that spark their imaginations. Rough drawings elicit feedback that helps the team discover the spirit of the home building or renovation project ahead. Not only does this early learning process aid in creating preliminary plans, but it also helps develop the mutual trust so necessary for a dynamic and successful experience.

While this process is conducted primarily to teach the team about its client, it inevitably becomes a two-way street. For instance, when it's time to select new materials, team members have the opportunity to explain to the client the differences and benefits of one option over another. This takes considerable pressure off the clients. The responsibilities are no longer theirs alone. When the pressure is off, they make better, more visionary decisions, and have a more enjoyable time in the process.

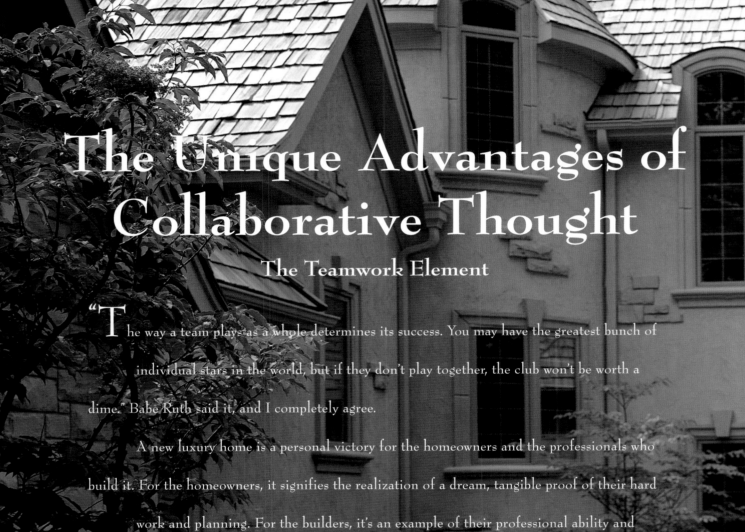

The Unique Advantages of Collaborative Thought

The Teamwork Element

"The way a team plays as a whole determines its success. You may have the greatest bunch of individual stars in the world, but if they don't play together, the club won't be worth a dime." Babe Ruth said it, and I completely agree.

A new luxury home is a personal victory for the homeowners and the professionals who build it. For the homeowners, it signifies the realization of a dream, tangible proof of their hard work and planning. For the builders, it's an example of their professional ability and originality that will stand on the land for many generations.

The home is, indeed, a personal victory for each individual involved, but even more, it is the end result of a total team effort.

"*Design and build firms assemble a team of consummate experts. It's our job as builders. It just makes sense.*

We're there from beginning to end anyway, so why wouldn't we take the responsibility for assembling the team?"

Orren Pickell

A design/build team runs smoothly, professionally, and, above all, creatively, because it functions as one focused unit. Because the team members work for the same company, the "finger pointing" that can take place when independent professionals are working on a home just doesn't happen. In design/build, the architect surely won't blame a cost overrun on the contractor. The landscape professionals won't cut down a tree and blame the architect for not telling him the tree was meant to stay. The interior designer doesn't mistakenly order a dining room table too large to fit into the room and blame the mistake on the contractor. Instead, regular, consistent communication among professionals all but eliminates these kinds of mistakes. Clients can remain focused on the project, always learning, always contributing, always comfortable.

The trimmed arch in this living room is a difficult-to-achieve and absolutely SPECTACULAR *feature—another example of what can be accomplished when all the elements of the home building process are working together.*

Dennis Ward, *Executive Vice President, Construction*

"There were so many people involved in the making of this room. The spirit of

teamwork *created by the design/build approach is unmatched."*

Richard Menna, Richard Menna Interior Design

•49•

"Every time I look at this house, I see a true testament to the power of teamwork. Every angle, every landscaped corner, the dramatic impact of its curb appeal, not to mention the beauty and quality *of the interior, all came together to satisfy the clients' lifetime desire for a unique luxury lifestyle."*

Wendy Cohen

"A design/build *approach offers clients the perfect opportunity to really analyze how they want to live. They get input from a team of designers from the very beginning. The collaboration yields incredible ideas which are turned into beautiful, flexible, and customized living spaces — indoors and out."*

Orren Pickell

"Builders are the captains of their teams, and I really enjoy my responsibility in that role. It's a pleasure *to meet so many successful and smart clients. And professionally, I couldn't ask for better opportunities to create beautiful homes. But honestly, without the individuals that work with me, I would not achieve anywhere near this level of quality. I strongly believe in the team."*

Orren Pickell

"A harmonious work environment results in a harmonious *design.*

We think this kitchen is perfect — it's exactly what the homeowner wanted."

John Troxell, *Wood-Mode Fine Custom Cabinetry*

"Home automation *is no longer just as 'nice option' to have — it's a way to protect your investment."*

Dave Kapor, *Paul Heath Audio & Video*

Teamwork is a concept that will continue to grow in acceptance and popularity in the 21st

century. Business executives, university professors, professional athletes, and two-

income families embrace it. The pace, the possibilities, and the competition of modern life

demand it. There are simply too many things to do in a short amount of time. A team

approach to building a home allows clients the time to participate at levels that their daily lives

can support.

I strongly believe that nobody is as smart

or as inventive as everybody. No

matter how many years of experience I can

bring to the team, no matter how

many homes our architects have designed,

no matter how many times our

client has built a new home, we need each

other's insight, wisdom, and spirit

of innovation. And in design/build firms,

the process for working as a team is

built in. We are convinced that as years go

by, more and more home building

customers are going to demand

a solid team approach for their

project, because they understand its

financial and creative values. Their

jobs often involve working on teams, and their children are learning about teamwork and team

spirit as students and athletes. As a result, they will increasingly demand that their

builders work in experienced teams.

Teamwork is and will be the element that drives the success of most every custom home

building or remodeling project.

The Vision
The Creative Design Element

Initially, a site for the house is selected. This is the most fundamental, and possibly the most important, step in the custom home building process. It is also one of the most complex. It all starts with location, location, location — the city, the neighborhood within the city, and the home site within the neighborhood. That is also the order of their importance. After schools, city services, taxes, shopping, and proximity to the client's job are considered and the city is chosen, it is the responsibility of the sales team to help the client find the right area, or neighborhood, within the city. This is a basic real estate decision and, in the end, it is based primarily upon the client's tastes. Finally, the piece of land must be decided upon. At this point, the design/build team becomes involved. Several dozen items — topography, landscape, distance from the street, drainage, price, size, hills, lakes — are considered. They will often define the scope, style, and character of the home.

Once the site is chosen and purchased, the design team walks the site, often at a quiet time. I find early mornings are best. At this point, the house is only a hazy vision of the client's imagination. The team begins to envision rooms and views that take advantage of hills, high and low points, grand views, and proximity to lakes, streams, ravines, or forests.

Next, the architects begin their magic, and the homeowner's lifelong dreams are transformed into creative expressions. They assume a form, a shape, and a life of their own.

Good design is the defining element of all successful home-building or remodeling projects. It's the element that allows for creative innovation. It brings unique concepts to life, and introduces the little details that the homeowner will relish for years to come. This is where design/build professionals and clients work together to practice the art of seeing the invisible, of creating something fresh, new, and wonderful.

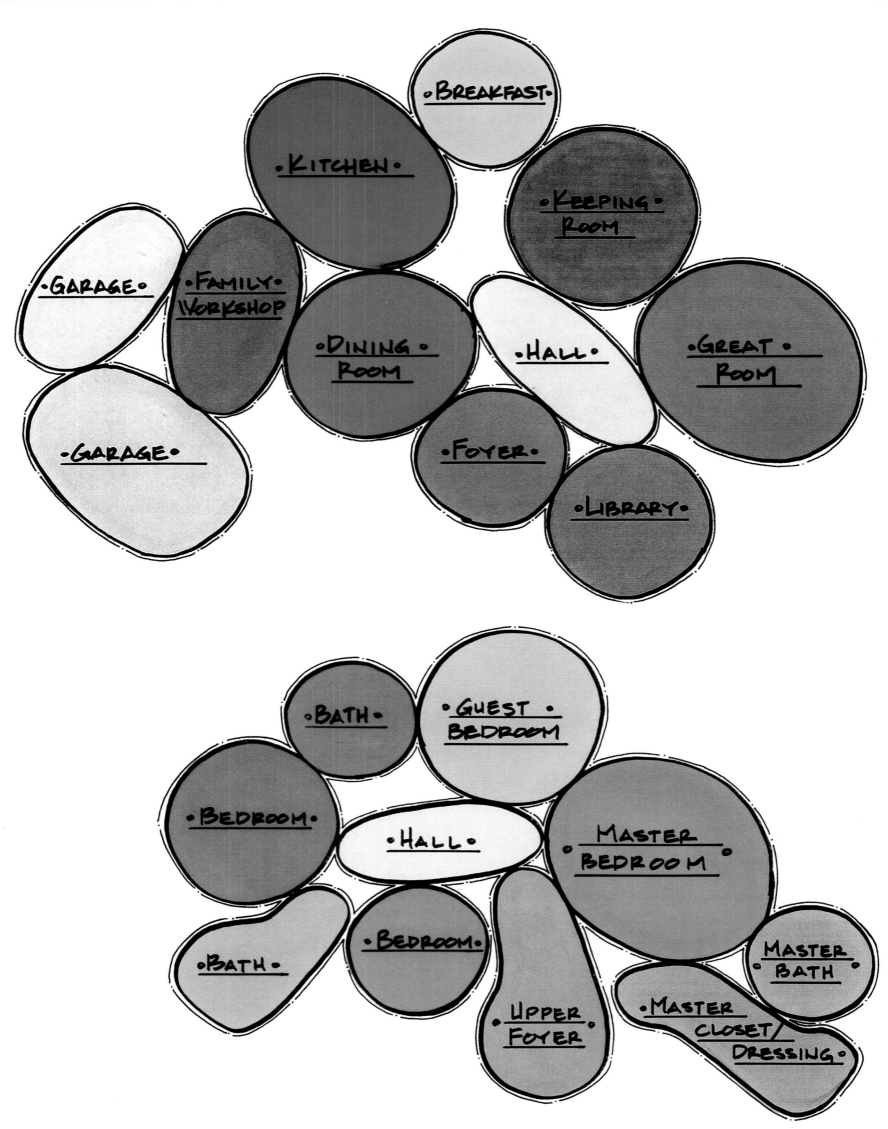

"Bubble diagrams like these are drawn at initial meetings between the architectural team and the homeowners. These

flexible, loose, rough sketches serve as the visual *cue that suggests the direction a floor plan will eventually take."*

Orren Pickell

"Architects think about their projects all the time. For example, I'll be watching my daughter's recital when a neat detail for the home I'm currently working on pops into my mind. I preserve the idea on a napkin, or other easily available scratch paper, until I get back to my office and add it to the formal drawing. Many **wonderful** *ideas have been born from a scribble on a scrap of paper."*

Tony Perry

These "napkin drawings" as they're known in the architectural profession, aren't used to communicate with clients, but to keep the architect's creative juices flowing during the design process. Design professionals just grab the closest napkin, matchbook cover, or Post-It®, and record a brainstorm idea while it's clear and fresh in their minds. It's a practice that's been recorded in architectural lore. There are even napkin drawing competitions in the architectural profession. Even in the information age, one can't improve on this idea!

The client is, of course, intimately involved in the architectural planning process. Here is where their childhood fantasies, as well as their adult requirements, are discussed. Ideas flow freely in creative brainstorming sessions. This first taste of synergy is exhilarating — the ideas are exciting, and often better than anything the client could have dreamed of alone.

The meetings usually take place over a 2-3 month period. The design team must be very good listeners during this process, interpreting not only the client's words, but also his and her *feelings*. To give the clients a starting point and a tangible visual reference, architects first visit the site and make rough drawings of the home. At this point, the sketches are simple bubble drawings, but that changes quickly. They brainstorm with the clients, brainstorm among themselves, create more refined renderings, and brainstorm with the clients again. By this point, a dozen architects may have offered ideas and recommendations. The next set of drawings usually comes very close to the final plan. The most progressive firms have begun to create videotapes of computer-generated virtual reality "fly-bys", both inside and outside the house (even the landscaping is included!), to give the clients a more complete view of how their new home will look and flow. Samples are shown in this chapter. With a few final

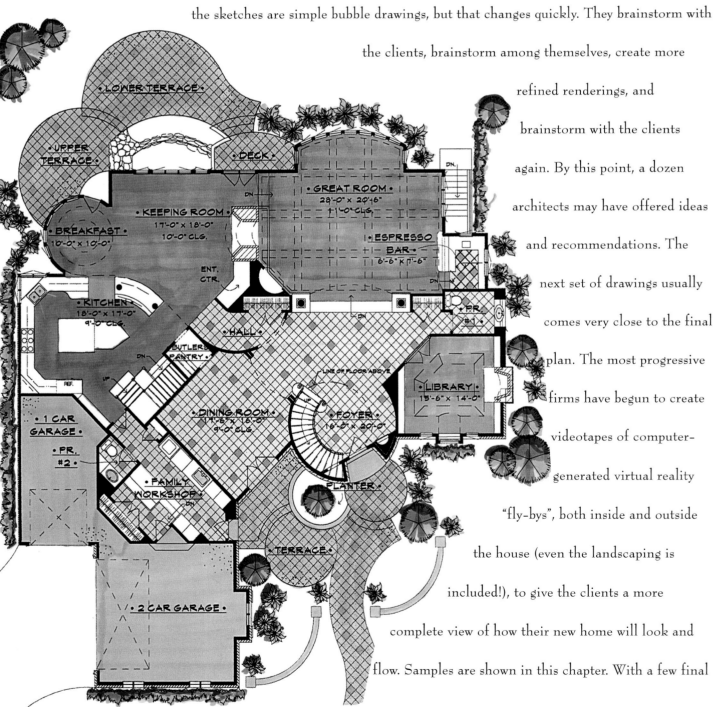

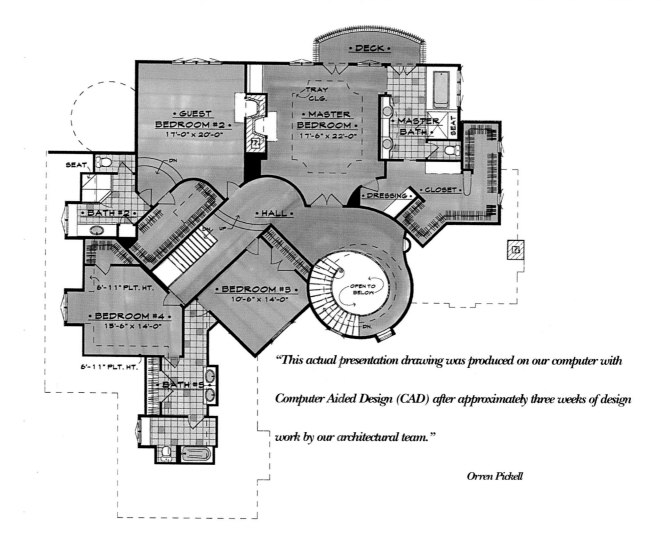

personal touches from the client, the design is complete. On paper, the process sounds tedious, but believe me, it is thrilling and highly creative for everyone involved!

Then begins the *selections* process. Before it ends, it will involve literally thousands of decisions by the homeowner. What color and type of roof? What tile for the kitchen floor? The master bathroom? What faucets in what finishes in what rooms? What lighting, room by room? Whirlpools, steamrooms, hot tubs, entertainment centers, libraries, landscaping...the choices never seem to end, and can sometimes be overwhelming. That's why there is no substitute for a good interior designer during the selections process. Find an interior designer (or let your design/build firm recommend one) and listen to him/her. This person's responsibilities go way beyond wall coverings, draperies, and furniture fabrics...they involve helping the client make key decisions, keeping the process moving, and in the end, building the home on schedule.

A good interior designer doesn't *cost* money; he or she *saves* money. Not to mention time and anxiety!

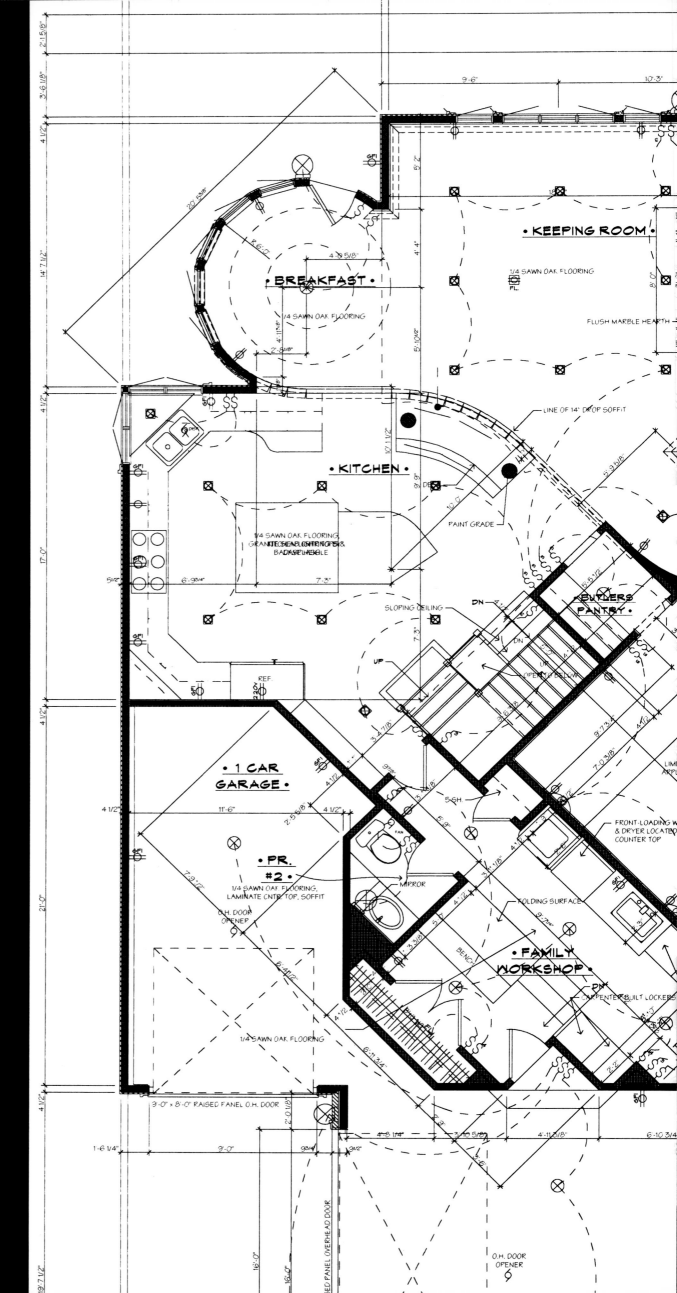

"This is the floor plan of the same house. You can see how this evolved *from the bubble drawings on the previous pages. Each step forward in the design process creates another level of excitement for the client and the staff as we move from the planning stages toward construction."*

Tony Perry

· KEEPING ROOM ·

1/4 SAWN OAK FLOORING

FLUSH MARBLE HEARTH

· BREAKFAST ·

1/4 SAWN OAK FLOORING

LINE OF 14" DROP SOFFIT

· KITCHEN ·

PAINT GRADE

1/4 SAWN OAK FLOORING, GRANITE COUNTER TOP & BACKSPLASH

SLOPING CEILING

· BUTLERS PANTRY ·

DN

DN

UP

REF.

· 1 CAR GARAGE ·

FRONT-LOADING W & DRYER LOCATED COUNTER TOP

· PR. #2 ·

1/4 SAWN OAK FLOORING, LAMINATE CNTR. TOP, SOFFIT

MIRROR

FOLDING SURFACE

O.H. DOOR OPENER

BENCH

· FAMILY WORKSHOP ·

DN

CARPENTER BUILT LOCKERS

1/4 SAWN OAK FLOORING

3'-0" x 8'-0" RAISED PANEL O.H. DOOR

RAISED PANEL OVERHEAD DOOR

O.H. DOOR OPENER

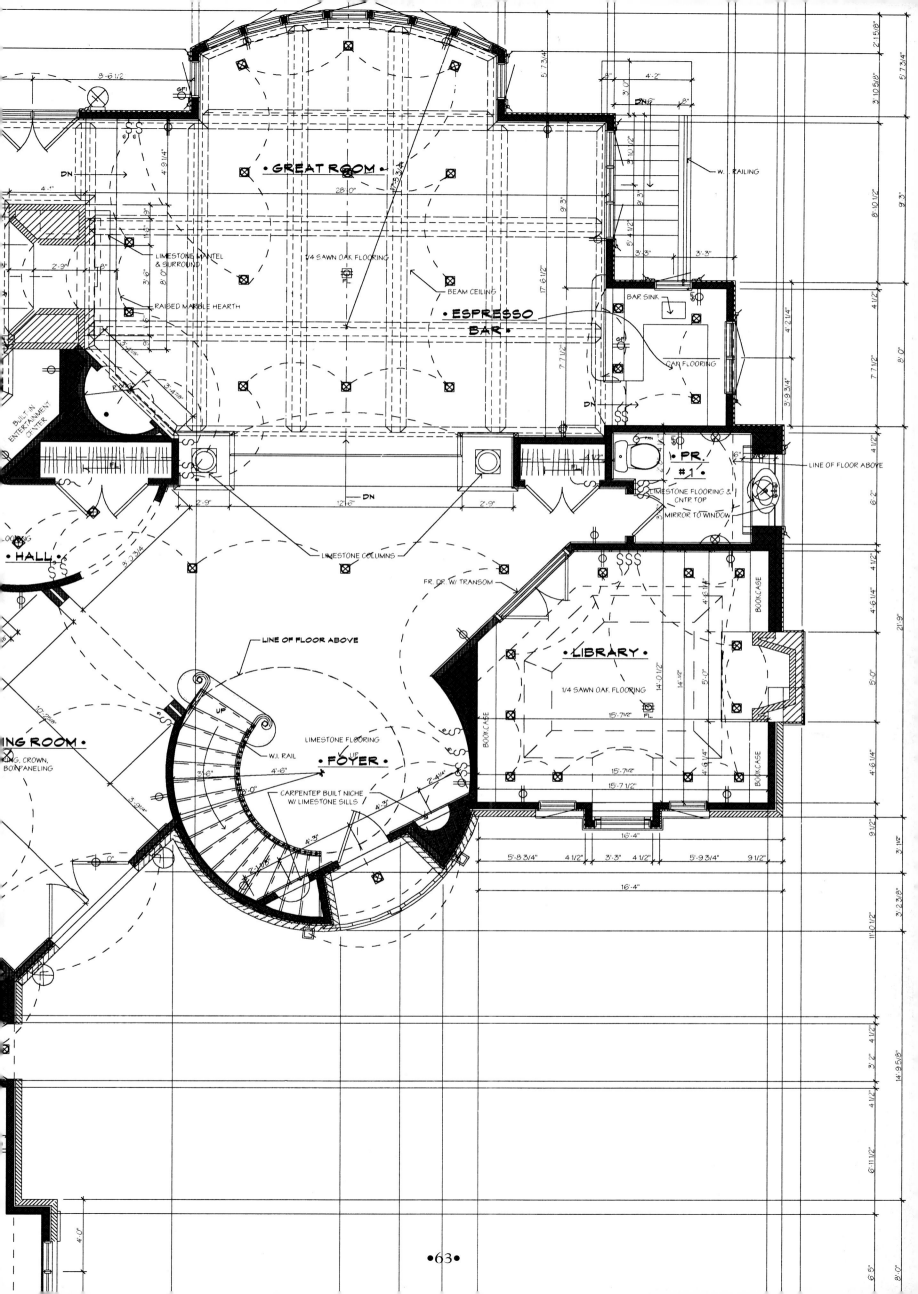

• GREAT ROOM •
28'-0"

LIMESTONE MANTEL
& SURROUND

RAISED MARBLE HEARTH

1/4 SAWN OAK FLOORING

BEAM CEILING

• ESPRESSO
BAR •

BAR SINK

OAK FLOORING

W. RAILING

DN

BUILT-IN
ENTERTAINMENT
CENTER

DN

• PR.
#1 •

LIMESTONE FLOORING &
CNTR. TOP

MIRROR TO WINDOW

LINE OF FLOOR ABOVE

• HALL •

2'-9"   2'-9"
12'-6"
DN

LIMESTONE COLUMNS

FR. DR. W/ TRANSOM

• LIBRARY •

1/4 SAWN OAK FLOORING

15'-7 1/2"
FL.

BOOKCASE

BOOKCASE

LINE OF FLOOR ABOVE

ING ROOM •

NG, CROWN,
BOX PANELING

UP

W.I. RAIL

• FOYER •

UP

LIMESTONE FLOORING

CARPENTER BUILT NICHE
W/ LIMESTONE SILLS

4'-6"
3'-6"

15'-7 1/2"
15'-7 1/2"

5'-8 3/4" 4 1/2" 3'-3" 4 1/2" 5'-9 3/4" 9 1/2"
16'-4"
16'-4"

"Although this preliminary drawing is purposely loose and sketchy, clients get a thrill out of seeing their dream home come to life. If we've done our job right, we're already very close to fulfilling *that dream."*

Orren Pickell

"This is the rendered drawing of the same house. Before we take it this far, our entire architectural team, about a dozen professionals, have studied the plan and made their suggestions. When it pleases all of us, the client usually loves *it too."*

Tony Perry

Twenty-first century home building projects will be enhanced by the power of

technology. Computer programs allow homeowners to see their plans

come alive in 3-D animation (displayed on the next couple of pages). With this

tool, architects can show clients a variety of possibilities for any room or

landscape area. With a quick click, clients can see their landscape in any season,

with annual flowers or flowering bushes, and all varieties of walkways and

lighting. The technology can even insert representations of the children's bicycles

to make the scenes seem more realistic.

By leveraging the latest technologies, up-to-date design/build firms shave

weeks off the design process and offer their clients exciting opportunities

to actually see their visions come alive.

These CAD images are produced by a computer tool to show clients exact representations of their home before the first brick is laid at the homesite. If a banister looks overpowering, it's easy to try different sizes of newels, or smaller railings.

One of the more popular features of this CAD program is its ability to completely personalize the presentation. For instance, the animator can put a family's own furniture in a room, and even put their pottery and pictures on the bookshelves.

The design team appreciates the technology. It answers questions before they get to the costly point of learning onsite. If a client wants a detail that our team isn't sure about, they first model it on the computer. And, the construction team first sees landscaping and hardscapes on the fly-by.

When interiors and exteriors come alive in animation, every member of the team feels the excitement of creation. Clients virtually "walk through" the kitchen or around the yard. It's a chance to actually see the house and make changes. Also, it's thrilling!

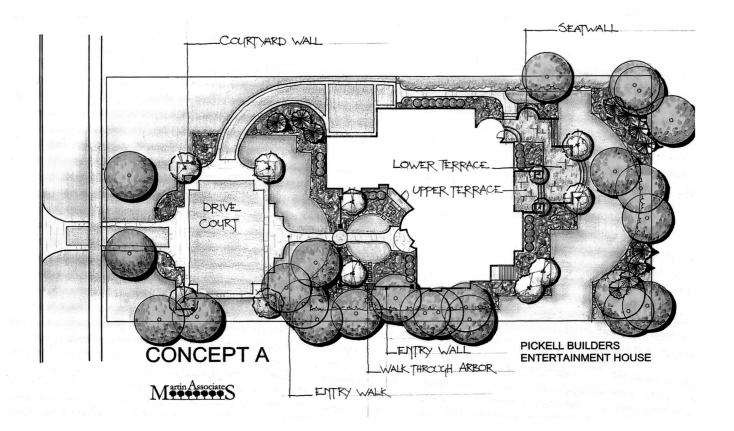

COURTYARD WALL

SEATWALL

LOWER TERRACE

UPPER TERRACE

DRIVE COURT

CONCEPT A

Martin Associates

ENTRY WALL

WALK THROUGH ARBOR

ENTRY WALK

PICKELL BUILDERS
ENTERTAINMENT HOUSE

World-class homes deserve to be set in exciting landscapes that enhance the beauty of the architecture while enriching the lives of the clients. An essential part of the design team, landscape architects are involved in the design process from the conceptual stages through to the completion of a project.

By working closely with clients to establish long-term relationships, landscape architects learn to appreciate the client's specific goals and dreams. These visions are incorporated into the development of multiple design concepts and are a source of discussion and excitement. Together with the landscape architect, the client chooses a more specific design course to follow, and the final landscape plans are then developed for review and refinement.

The design and layout of every part of the landscape — from driveways and walks to pools and planting beds — is inspired by the client's goals and dreams and given form by the landscape architect's creativity and expertise.

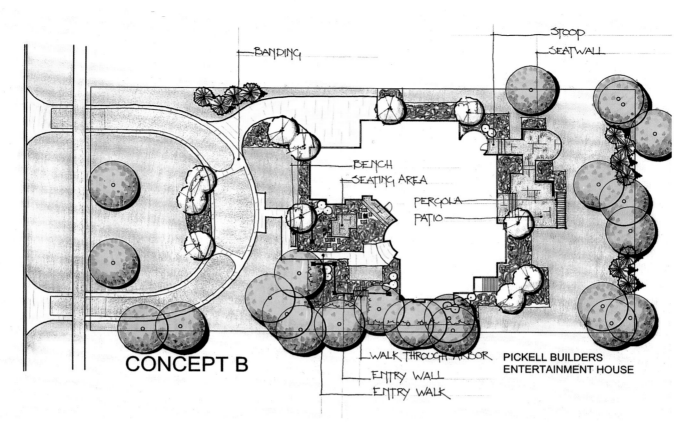

BANDING

STOOP
SEATWALL

BENCH
SEATING AREA

PERGOLA
PATIO

CONCEPT B

WALK THROUGH ARBOR

ENTRY WALL
ENTRY WALK

PICKELL BUILDERS
ENTERTAINMENT HOUSE

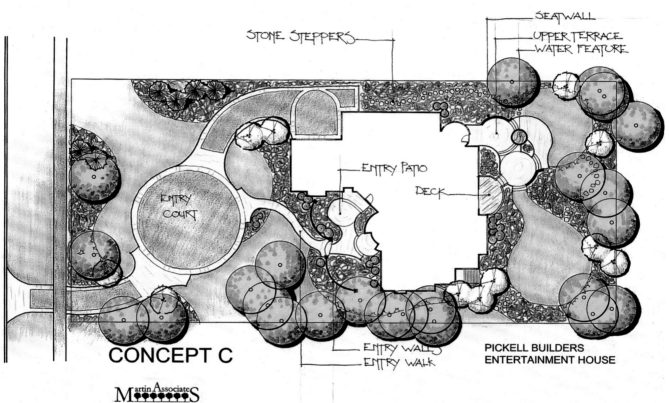

STONE STEPPERS

SEATWALL
UPPER TERRACE
WATER FEATURE

ENTRY PATIO
DECK

ENTRY
COURT

CONCEPT C

ENTRY WALL
ENTRY WALK

PICKELL BUILDERS
ENTERTAINMENT HOUSE

Martin Associates

"The client was so happy with the design of the added

water feature. The waterfall cascades into the spa and

recirculates. We love to hear the client's ideas. There are

so many things we can do to bring existing landscaping

up to a higher level of enhancement."

Thomas C. Bolas, *Martin Associates Landscaping*

Building on Experience
The Project Management Element

There are hundreds of decisions to be made in the process of building a new home. How well these decisions are tracked — what's been done, what's left to be done, and how one decision impacts another — is often what distinguishes the great creative experience from the frustrating project. Project management, ensuring that projects are completed on time and on budget, according to their design requirements, is critical.

Project Management is the formal process of tracking decisions and responsibilities throughout the home building project.

The selections process was mentioned earlier. Suffice it to say, clients need to make many hundreds of decisions, and those decisions need to be acted upon, prior to breaking ground. Hundreds more occur after the building process begins — and this doesn't include changes that occur along the way! Also, a timeline needs to be set in place and adhered to, lest time and money be extended beyond reasonable and acceptable points. For the sake of the client, it is imperative that a system to manage all this be implemented.

The systems used in the Project Management process are aided by the design/build approach (since all phases of design and construction are controlled through a single office) and made more accurate and flexible by ever-more sophisticated software. These computer tools guide clients to make decisions, keep on schedules, and stay within their budgets. They keep everybody happy and the project on track.

The next great project management tool will be accessed via your home computer, using the Internet and your design/build firm's web site. Clients can access the web site using a personal access code. They will then be able to view the progress of their home according to the pre-established timeline. Not only will the budget be constantly accessible, but it will change instantly as your selections change. The items available for selection can be viewed individually or side by side. The client will see color-accurate, high-resolution photos. In a few years, animated 3D software will be advanced enough to instantly show the exact sink and faucets you have picked, along with your cabinets, knobs, tiles, paint, wallpaper, and lighting, as they will actually appear in your kitchen!

"This wonderful *island was custom-built to meet the needs of the homeowners. Its finish gives it a furniture look, while it includes such*

features as a secondary vegetable sink, dishwasher, wine cooler, and lowered butcher block counter. Good project management ensures that strong

lines of communication flow between all members of the design/build team. It results in extraordinary and unique touches, like this kitchen."

Dave Heigl

...is a multi-purpose, fun space designed for the family's young son. As you can see, there are many

construction and design elements at work: specialized flooring, built-in cabinetry, a custom headboard,

and the window seat that doubles as an extra bed for impromptu 'sleep-overs.'

Keeping track of all of these items would have been a nightmare without our management tools."

Orren Pickell

Clients usually experience an anxious period when the timelines of their preliminary plans are completed and deadlines are upon them. Suddenly, they feel crushed by the weight of time commitments.

To help assure them that this sequence of events is normal, and that the project is, indeed, being closely controlled and moving forward, design/builders carefully outline the process for their clients. At regular meetings, timelines and budgets are presented and reviewed. Though creating a custom-built home is a fluid, ever-changing "artist's canvas" with a life of its own, good communication and planning eliminate most surprises.

The best design/build firms are committed to keeping client interest high. This translates into a more dedicated, involved client who is motivated enough to maintain the important schedule of deadlines and decision making. Clients who have a fascination with the process seem to always be the happiest.

Client communication and project planning are the bedrocks of a successful custom-built home, and they free architect, builder, and client from their creative inhibitions. Great homes follow, on time and on budget.

"This foyer, with its stained glass doors and Prairie-inspired trim detail, makes a dramatic *first impression."*

Orren Pickell

"Modern management tools are vital for the uninterrupted flow of the project. They keep everyone ORGANIZED *and on track. When there are questions, we have reliable documents to refer to."*

Tony Perry

"The meticulous workmanship that went into the installation if this incredible *bathroom is evident. Without the experienced, careful craftsmen who did this job, our designs would not have been so completely realized. Their parts in the process are crucial to success."*

Dennis Ward

Clients who seek design/build firms to custom build their luxury homes are much more than just financially successful people. After all, there are plenty of large homes already available. These are intense, high-energy people, the movers and shakers of our society, extremely bright and often well-educated, holding the highest positions with the most responsibilities.

So one can understand that they are extremely busy. Architects and contractors struggle to find ever-more reliable Project Management tools, to let these clients conserve their time and enjoy their home building projects. Technology has certainly helped. Computer hardware is becoming more robust, software more sophisticated, and Internet capabilities much faster. As our clients embrace these communication technologies, design/builders gain the opportunities to streamline their processes and better serve them. Everyone benefits, everyone saves time and money, and, in the end, the best quality home is built.

The shortest distance between two points is a straight line, and that's what design/build is all about: A straight line between the client and the professional team. That is the future of luxury home building in the 21st century.

Craftsmanship at the Highest Level

Honoring The Construction Element

The moment has come to begin building the dream. There is no more exciting time in the process, and few creative experiences in life can match it. (Love and the love of children are obvious exceptions!) For six months to a year or more, you watch a piece of land become transformed. A giant hole in the ground is dug, filled with concrete, steel, timber, masonry, glass, plaster, or all of the above. And, with the skills, energies, and determinations of dozens of master craftsmen, it comes to life and becomes your home — from the faint, shadowy memories of your childhood to a vivid, tangible edifice that you and your family can enjoy every single day for the rest of your lives. For me, there's just nothing like it.

So, grab a hammer and some nails, and let's explore the construction phase and honor the craftsmen who make it all happen.

"Having top craftsmen *on our team allowed us to create a look for this home that was contemporary without the stark, bleak look that some contemporary homes can have. The rounded areas add shadow and light and result in a beautiful, soft effect."*

Dennis Ward

Your architect remains your confidant and supporter, but the Project

Superintendent has become your best friend. Welcome to the

construction phase of the design/build experience.

Now you will watch a group of committed people dedicate themselves to their

daily work and, with their hands, minds, and raw sinew, create what

most individuals simply cannot: a finest quality, luxury home.

From raw materials of the earth,

they build sleek floors, elegant

rounded arches, and sweeping

staircases. They lay stone tiles

above the granite countertops in your

perfect new kitchen...they

complete the giant whirlpool and steam

room/sit-down shower in your

new master bath...they painstakingly

hand-craft the fine mahogany bookcases in your elegant home library.

When the dust settles and they have completed their work, you might stand

across a lake, look back at your new home, and realize the genius and

the gift that is the American master craftsman.

"It's hard to choose my favorite feature of this living room, with its beam ceiling details,

limestone fireplace and columns, art niche with custom lighting, and barrel vault

ceiling. It demonstrates craftsmanship at the highest level.

Orren Pickell

"This swimming pool and Jacuzzi drew raves. It's such a casual atmosphere, yet every detail is so carefully thought out. The limestone floor was brought in piece by piece from Europe...*each stone was dated, set, and laid. The cedar ceiling and the stone fireplace complement each other beautifully. What an outstanding achievement."*

Tony Perry

"When I meet customers for the first time, they're always impressed by the design/build concept, if they haven't heard of it before. It's still pretty unusual to have all talents talking to each other and being orchestrated *in one place. It's business combined with art."*

Wendy Cohen

Exciting though it is, homeowners frequently feel vulnerable during the construction period. Tangible things are happening now, things that cannot be changed with the click of a mouse or the eraser end of a pencil.

Synergy is a word often abused in the business press. If you want to see real synergy in action, don't look to corporate mergers or new management techniques. Look to skilled, talented construction crews. As long as they are true to the architectural plans, a team of a dozen or more people can (and do) create wonderful end-products out of basic materials, tools, and human effort.

That elegant new kitchen? It's difficult to believe that a year ago, it was an overgrown lot. Those dotted lines on the architectural plans? Today, they're electric lines powering the recessed lights in a dramatic new family room. That timeline? It became a real thing, weeks and months that fell into place, according to plan and within budget.

And in the end, construction crews built the kitchen, pulled the electrical wires, installed the lighting cans, and kept to the schedule, day after day. The Superintendent adjusted plans and timelines according to minor (and sometimes major) client changes. Trucks rumbled in and out, and then one day, the noise stopped. The house was built and became a proud addition to the neighborhood and an important part of the client's life.

The Lasting Rewards of Commitment to Quality

The Element of Continuing Service

One of my favorite business terms is the "cult of the customer." It is an attitude that service-oriented companies have toward clients, an attitude that puts customer value at the top of the list. The managers and employees of these companies believe that their success is measured by their customer's satisfaction. In successful design/build firms, the "cult of the customer" is a founding concept of the company. Architects and builders go into business together because they recognize that it's an approach that offers the best value to their clients.

As we contemplate the value of design/build at the turn of the century, it is impossible not to factor in the worldwide trend toward the customization of products and services. We have evolved from an economy based upon mass-production to one predicated on individualized merchandise and service. I can order a one-of-a-kind chandelier to my exact specifications online this afternoon. So can you.

Clients expect and deserve direct, personal attention and service. The concept of an arrogant, self-important artist/craftsman is long dead. It's our job to cater to our clients, not vice-versa. Design/build firms go out of their ways to find and hire people at every level who are obsessed with client value and satisfaction.

This impacts the look and character of custom built, luxury homes, inside and out. First floor bedrooms and master bedrooms are built to accommodate elderly parents and aging baby boomers. Whirlpools, hot tubs, saunas, and steam rooms are commonplace, easing the

stress of hardworking clients. The "Bijou Palace" you saw on the proceeding pages is a fabulous home entertainment center. Such splendid, state-of-the-art, audio/visual rooms are directly tied to client demands, as they reach out to keep children, family, and friends together in this fast-paced, ever-changing culture. The billiard room and wet bar on this page and the party room on the next two pages represent more of the same. (Both of these are lower level rooms — basements— and are examples of excellent utilization of space.) Elegant swimming pools give families the chance to play together and exercise rooms allow hard-driving executive families to work out when they can, in the privacy of their homes. Vaulted garage areas double as indoor basketball courts. Libraries crafted in rich woods, with large windows that invite gracious, soft, natural lighting offer a respite from the demands of this computerized society.

Design/builders are well aware of the "high tech/high touch" needs of our clients and their families. Because we are with them throughout the entire building process, we get to know them. We know their kids, their interests, their tastes, and their dreams. It's all part of custom building their home, something every design/builder is passionate about.

"One of the best parts of my job is the parties! It's not uncommon for our clients to throw a party in conjunction with the date of their one year closing for the team that designed and built the house. We get the opportunity to see them enjoying their home, and showing it off to their friends."

Wendy Cohen

We're proud *of the work we do and the effects we achieve. Design/builders do whatever it takes to find out what the client is looking for and to make it happen. "*

Orren Pickell

Be sure that any design/build company you're considering has a strong record of

customer service excellence. It's pretty simple to check out. Start by requesting a

list of current and past clients. The company should be more than happy to provide it.

When you call these references, ask specific questions regarding the levels of

service during each phase of the project, and after the project was completed. If you're

invited to visit the house, take that as a signal that the customer was very happy

with the service, the outcome, and the entire experience.

Visit a few of the current job sites. They should be professionally maintained and

controlled.

Finally, trust your intuition. Team members should seem intensely interested in your

wants, needs, and desires, as well as those of your family. They should be great

listeners, so they can learn about your experiences, tastes, and dreams. Not every builder

is the same, so it's worth the legwork to find a company that will fit your

personal style and service requirements.

People who can build a luxury home or add a fabulous addition haven't succeeded by

accident. They're smart. They're savvy. They work hard. They know what good

service is. They expect it. They deserve it.

"*Our* commitment *to customer service carries through long past the move-*

in date. The quality of our work is second to none. Why shouldn't we stand behind it?

Dennis Ward

Spinning the Cocoon
Ever Cozier
The Element of the Future

Clients are smarter, more sophisticated, and better educated than ever. But they're
busier than any generation of luxury homeowners I've ever built for. The pace of
their lives and their desire for a peaceful, protected environment are often the first
things they talk about. The longing for this "cocoon" is often their strongest
emotion. "Cozy, comfortable, and safe" will be the defining characteristics of luxury
homes in the 21st century.

"When the kitchen environment reflects the look and feel of the rest of the house, it creates a sense of harmony *that reinforces the pleasurable experience of living there."*

Janice Stone Thomas, *ASID, CKD, Wood-Mode Fine Custom Cabinetry*

The trend towards cocooning — the desire to make a home an insulated, safe haven, has been evident for the past ten years. The emergence of the Great Room, the transformation of the kitchen into the heart of the home, the growing interest in gardens, a renewed commitment to environmentally conscious design and materials...these are all examples of cocooning influencing the design and building of a home.

Home is no longer just a showplace: it's the center of family life, where people live, work, and nurture one another. Many clients no longer want to build a dining room that will only be used quarterly (one evening every three months). Nor do they want a formal living room, even if they do have a collection of Heirloom-quality art or furniture. Instead, they invest in the "jewel box" trend. That is, they live in 100% of their home on a weekly basis. Rarely used areas are eliminated. Rooms are optimally sized and their levels of finish — their architectural detailings — are drastically increased.

"The doors and the glass are uniquely curved — they were put there to provide a stunning *view of the garden. The floor is made of concentric oak circles laid in individually. The design of this room was a dream — a concept come to life."*

Richard Menna, *Richard Menna Interior Design*

"In the future, *space for its own sake will be less important, as energy and environmentally conscious clients opt for the 'jewel box' instead of the 'jewelry store' approach to comfortable living."*

Orren Pickell

"Functional and practical landscape design solutions *must be developed to meet the individual needs*

of our clients. However, it is the careful integration of architecture and landscape — through thoughtful selection

of materials and plantings — that ultimately create a successful combination of beauty and utility."

James P. Martin, *Landscape Architect, Martin Associates Landscaping*

"When a person drives up the driveway of his or her home after a day at work or extended business trip, or a few hours of running errands, a feeling of serenity *is already embracing them. That is, if we've done our job right."*

Dennis Ward

Also, the modern luxury home comes equipped with fax machines, copiers, computer networks, and telecommunication devices. Distributed audio and video systems, as well as custom-built home theaters, are transforming the home into the family's primary place of entertainment. Parents yearn to provide a safe, fun environment for their children, and ultimately, their grandchildren.

Families are becoming conscious of the importance of spending quality time together, in the most wonderful, enjoyable, safe place anywhere, and design/builders are creating their homes accordingly.

As the 21st century unfolds, homeowners will weave the cocoon even cozier. The unpredictability of the world will make a secure home seem even more important and home security systems will grow in popularity. We'll continue to see intense interest in "smart homes," those wired for remote control of lights, appliances, and even window treatments. Homeowners are demanding total (but always user-friendly) control of their environments...at their fingertips. Designing and installing meticulously crafted home automation systems is more than a specialized skill, it's an art. Think how good it would feel to close your drapes and turn on the front light from miles away, should you decide to have dinner in the city. Consider pre-heating the oven from your car, on your way home from carpooling. Design/builders will partner with electronic architects, ensuring that today's dream homes will more than hold their values, long into the New Millennium.

Bathrooms and master bedrooms, the luxury zones of the cocoon, offer the total quiet and relaxation people crave. They're tired of the health club, so they build a private retreat to serve as a custom fitness and wellness center. Soothing showers or tubs, sitting areas, built-in refrigerators, meditation rooms, and a quiet space for a massage are popular features of the ultimate at-home environment.

The availability of high-quality home entertainment and office systems defines the cocoon. As I mentioned earlier, entertainment centers have become great multi-media areas, drawing families together. The old adage that "a family that plays together, stays together" doesn't sound so old-fashioned anymore! Homeowners are enthusiastically installing home theaters with state-of-the-art systems.

Finally, clients are taking advantage of new work styles and embracing telecommuting, working at home whenever they can. The cocoon supports all their lifestyle choices.

A Grand Obsession

The Human Element

Exceptional design and construction standards are only two of three equal elements

of the home building project. The final component, in many ways the most

important, is the human element, that is, the experiences and personalities of the

design/build professionals, and the relationships they develop with their clients.

At the end of the day, those relationships are the foundations of the luxury

home building process.

"This is such a beautiful home—a great achievement.

We worked with the client to create the perfect blend of art and functionality.

We put in lots of windows for lots of light. The curves create shadows

and give the sleek, contemporary *home the softness*

that the client wanted."

Tony Perry

I like to walk the sites of future homes myself, to determine how the houses will best sit on the topographies and fit into the overall scenes. I often do this in the silence and soft hues of dawn. Sometimes, when cold evenings are followed by warm days, mists form over lakes and streams, in dips between hills, and across valleys. Custom designing/home building is my profession and my passion, and I can envision great houses on this land.

I look at the white fog and green hills, and I think about how fortunate I am. After all, next to a person's health, family, beliefs, and career, nothing is as important as his or her home. Like custom luxury home builders everywhere, my clients include the Who's Who of this area: Giants of American industry; surgeons and anesthesiologists who make life and death decisions every day; stockbrokers who affect the incomes of thousands of investors; judges and lawyers who determine the rules we all live by; celebrities who are our heroes; and entrepreneurs who are building the future of our economy. These people, these families, have entrusted their homes to me and the professionals who work with me.

Speaking for design/build professionals everywhere, this is a trust I take very seriously, and an honor that humbles me. Across America, remarkable homes have been and are being built. And this is just the dawn of the New Millennium.

"I think each home we do is a reflection *of the client's personality. We don't impress our own personal style upon the client — we take the client's own vision of the perfect home and bring it to fruition."*

Wendy Cohen

"Today's technological revolution in sound and picture quality is transforming the way families entertain themselves. The current home theater invites families, together with their friends, to enjoy an engrossing shared experience. Suddenly, staying at home becomes irresistible.*"*

Dave Kapov, Paul Heath Audio & Video

"More and more, people are seeing their homes as a haven, *a retreat from a busy world. It then becomes that much more important to make their home a beautiful, welcoming place."*

Dennis Ward

"It is important to our clients to have a kitchen that is not only beautiful,

but functional and comfortable."

Dave Heigl

"For most homeowners, building a custom home is the realization of a dream. So for us, the

process never gets old. Every new project is a fresh challenge, *and we welcome that*

challenge every time. We are in a unique position to fulfill those dreams. It's an honor."

Orren Pickell

A home is not just a physical structure. It is the foundation upon which people build their lives. All the elements of the design/build approach come together in a symphony of creativity and craftsmanship to create a reflection of each homeowner's personality and lifestyle.

We design/builders ensure that each home is a true fulfillment of the client's needs by being there, from start to finish and beyond. And the client is with us every step of the way. Clients relish their role in this process. It enriches the building experience and gives them an intimate sense of connection with their new home.

Most homes start out with a client's vision or dream of the perfect home. The design/build approach reaches for that dream and turns it into a stunning reality.

Orren Pickell worked his way through Bradley University by opening a painting and decorating business. He studied and mastered architecture and construction. After college, he transformed his decorating business into a remodeling company. In 1975, he built his first home, and he did the majority of this with his own two hands, from drawing the plans to pouring concrete to framing, drywalling, and trimming it. For years, he continued to build his own homes himself, gaining invaluable experience at the grass roots level. Obsessed with quality and customer service, he grew the business.

Today, Orren Pickell Designers & Builders is a 25-year-old company, the premier custom home design/build firm in the Chicago area. The business has evolved to include a number of divisions. The purpose of each division is to help create a better quality home and to provide better service and value to the client. The divisions include the custom home building group, the broker/site-location group, and the rough and trim carpentry group (which operate under the corporate umbrella, Orren Pickell Designers & Builders); the Design Group (architecture); the Remodeling Group (remodeling and maintenance); and CabinetWerks (Pickell's kitchen and bath cabinetry design/build company located in Lincolnshire, Illinois). Each step in the process is quality-controlled, so that the houses are built and maintained to the highest standards in the industry.

The corporation has won well over 100 awards for excellence in innovation, design, and construction. Mr. Pickell has been named Builder of the Year, CEO of the month by the Lake County (Illinois) Business Journal, and has been a featured speaker for years at the National Custom Builder Conference. In 1999, Orren Pickell Designers & Builders was named one of the top eight builders in America to work for by Builder Magazine.

Dennis Ward is a master craftsman and Executive Vice President of Orren Pickell Designers & Builders. A Vietnam veteran, Ward brings his Marine mentality, dedication, and commitment to every project. He commands the respect and fierce loyalty of the hundreds of employees and construction subcontractors who work for the company, and the sincere appreciation of every Pickell client. He will not accept less than the highest standards for Pickell houses and Pickell employees. This shows loud and clear in every finished home. In the end, the strength and determination of Dennis Ward make dream homes come true.

Anthony Perry is Vice President of Design, and a Partner in the Design Group. Perry is a licensed architect who has won numerous prestigious awards. Perry, who has been with Pickell since 1992, supervises all design projects for the company, and oversees the CAD drafting program with virtual reality walk throughs. The imagination, innovation, and energy in every design are direct reflections of Tony Perry's professionalism.

Wendy Cohen is Vice President of Sales and Marketing for Orren Pickell Designers & Builders. A licensed real estate broker, she is in charge of sales and marketing activities for all groups and facets of the company. A graduate of Michigan State University, Mrs. Cohen joined Pickell in 1991 and helped create the company's nationally recognized Custom Home series. Since then, she has led the sales and marketing department during the company's greatest growth years.

David Heigl is a Partner in CabinetWerks, Pickell's high-end kitchen design firm. Dave studied architecture at the University of Wisconsin in Milwaukee and was a master carpenter for fifteen years. He joined Orren Pickell Designers & Builders in 1991, as the head of the trim and millwork division. A Certified Kitchen Designer, Dave currently supervises a large staff and is in the upper 5% of the nation in Wood-Mode/Brookhaven fine cabinetry sales.